A LINC(
RAILWAY CENTRE

A. J. LUDLAM

Published by the
Lincolnshire Wolds Railway Society

Class O2 2-8-0 No 63977 runs over Wellowgate crossing in March 1963. *W. Gladwell.*

An aerial view of Grimsby in 1972. Town station is at the bottom centre of the photograph with Garden Street crossing to the right of the station. The impressive Yarborough Hotel stands next to the station. The line from Louth, Boston, Peterborough and Kings Cross goes off right just beyond Garden Street. The line to the docks and Cleethorpes continues up the picture. Docks station is just before the flyover and the Docks Offices just beyond. The three fish docks are to the top right. The Royal Dock is top centre; the Alexandra Dock is crossed by Corporation Bridge which was the terminus of the Grimsby-Immingham electric tramway.

ISBN 978-0-9926762-8-5

The Lincolnshire Wolds Railway Society would like to thank Alf Ludlam and Phil Eldridge for giving their time to compile this publication, to Leyland Penn, David Enefer, Tony Jones, Peter Clark and William Gladwell for their contributions, and to Allinson Print & Supplies for their support with the project.

Printed by Allinson Print & Supplies, Allinson House, Lincoln Way, Fairfield Industrial Estate, Louth, Lincolnshire LN11 0LS

Issue 1. Spring 2016.

CONTENTS

The first train to leave Grimsby bound for New Holland on 28th February, 1848. *Reproduced from the Illustrated London News, 15th April, 1848.*

Hollingworth's Mill, Cartergate with St James Church beyond in 1860. *Humberside Libraries*

The Royal Dock on the occasion of Queen Victoria's Diamond Jubilee in 1897.

INTRODUCTION

In the Domesday Book, in 1086, Grimsby was described as, "having a church with a priest, a mill worth four shillings yearly and a ferry worth five shillings per annum". In 1201 King John granted the town its first Royal Charter. For several centuries the town remained of relatively little importance, until the Grimsby Haven Company was formed in 1796. The company obtained Parliamentary Powers to "widen, deepen and generally improve the Haven". The result was the first enclosed dock, which was opened in 1801. It became known as the Old Dock and was later incorporated into the Alexandra Dock.

The towns of Grimsby, Cleethorpes and Immingham were all well known for different reasons. Grimsby, the biggest fishing port in the world; Cleethorpes as a seaside resort and Immingham for its commercial docks. None of them would have developed without the arrival of the Manchester, Sheffield & Lincolnshire Railway (MS&LR) in North Lincolnshire.

"The Railway Chronicle" on 4th March, 1848 described Grimsby as "a miserable collection of mean brick-built houses and ill painted streets", but it added, "Railways will amend this", continuing "In addition to the lines they (the MS&LR) have produced, at a moderate price, the Old Dock of Grimsby and long canal running into the town, they have also commenced the construction of a new dock from plans by Mr Rendel. One fact will give an idea of what Grimsby may expect to become. Five years ago Customs receipts were £200 less than expenses, in 1847 the clear profits over expenses were £70,000".

At its peak the dock area of Grimsby consisted of six docks with a total water area of 139 acres, a total length of quays of six miles and 81 miles of railway track.

When the Royal Dock was opened by Queen Victoria in 1852 it was the most modern commercial dock in the United Kingdom. Coal was exported and timber brought in, as well as butter from Scandinavia, at a time when refrigeration was in its early days. The Great Central railway (GCR) operated trains taking butter to Manchester in special refrigerated vans.

The Alexandra Dock opened in 1879 and was an extension of the old Haven Dock and the Union Dock that connected to the Royal Dock.

Designed to handle coal and timber, coal drops Nos 3 and 4 were built to load colliers with high-grade steam coal from the South Yorkshire coalfields. A busy branchline left the MS&LR main line where Macaulay Street school now stands, and ran north down what is now Boulevard Avenue, over the river Freshney and down Pyewipe Road to the coal drops. By 1910 2,715,479 tons of coal was being handled by Grimsby docks.

Due to housing development in the West Marsh at the beginning of the 20th century the branch was abandoned and a new connection constructed from West Marsh Junction. New large capacity coal hoists, fed by conveyor belts and capable of handling 1,600 tons an hour, made the coal handling facilities in the Alexandra Dock redundant in the 1930s.

The Alexandra Dock became the centre for timber imports with many local timber merchants building sawmills and drying sheds in the area. "Deal Carriers", with their trademark leather pads strapped to their shoulders upon which they balanced planks of wood and stacked them in piles on the quayside, were a familiar sight. The Union Dock was widened to enable car-carrying vessels to reach the new car terminal opened in May 1975 at the west end of the docks.

The first of three fish docks was opened in 1856 and the third in 1934.

Railway staff at Grimsby Docks in 1893, an interesting array of headgear on show.

2

Newmarket Street Bridge, Central Market end. Built in 1871 and seen here in 1872. The shop on the left was where generations of Grimsby natives bought their fruit and sweets before crossing Victoria Street to visit the Palace Theatre. A row of coal merchants and their carts are fronted by one belonging to E. Bannister, an old Grimsby firm.

A view of the fish docks taken from the Dock Tower on 29th September, 1934. The pontoon is seen running up the centre of the photo.

Fish Department clerical staff in 1893. Top row: Alf Grimble, W. R. Bullen, J. Pawson; bottom row: W. R. Pawson, C. H. Smith, W. R. Whitehouse, J. Davies, K. H. Higginbottom, W. R. Swallow, Williamson.

A view of Grimsby Docks station from the footbridge at Cleethorpe Road level crossing. *A. W. Croughton*

THE ARRIVAL OF THE RAILWAYS

The companies which formed the Manchester, Sheffield & Lincolnshire Railway, by the Act of Amalgamation on 27th July 1861, were the Sheffield, Ashton-under-Lyne and Manchester Railway, which was operational, the Great Grimsby & Sheffield Junction Railway and the Sheffield & Lincolnshire Junction Railway, both about to be constructed, and finally the oldest of them all, the Grimsby Docks Company.

In the early 1800s the port began to attract Baltic trade and cod fishers from the North Sea. However it was the discovery of the Grest Silver Pit, south of the Dogger Bank, which became supremely important to the trawlers upon which the plans to develop Grimsby were founded.

The fourteen miles of railway between Louth and Grimsby opened on the same day as the MS&LR's line to New Holland, 1st March, 1848. The Grimsby-Louth line was the first passenger carrying route to be operated by the Great Northern Railway (GNR). Trains from both companies ran between Louth and New Holland, by mutual agreement. Agreement was reached between the MS&LR and the GNR for the latter's trains to run into Town station, this was effected by a sharp curve extending from Catherine Street to Garden Street. GNR authority in Grimsby ceased at North and South Junctions on a triangle between the Docks and Town stations. The GNR reached its huge warehouse on the docks by virtue of running powers over the MS&LR, which entitled the GNR to run Cleethorpes excursions over the same lines.

Weelsby Road level-crossing and halt. The crossing was replaced by a subway in 1933.

5

Class B7 (GCR Q9) 4-6-0 No 1361 stands at Grimsby Dock station with a passenger train on 6th September, 1947. The guard on the left hand platform waits to give the "right away" to a Cleethorpes bound train. *V. R. Webster*

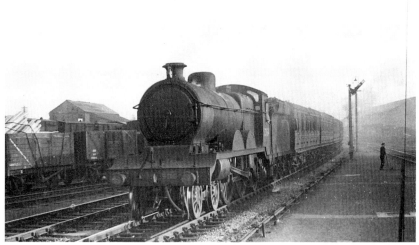

A New Holland to Cleethorpes passenger train approaches Grimsby Docks station, ex-GCR Compound Atlantic No 5364 "Lady Faringdon" in charge on 9th May, 1946. *H. C. Casserley*

LOGAN & HEMINGWAY

Between 1871 and 1880 the contractors Logan and Hemingway were involved in much work in the Grimsby area. This included repairs to and extensions of the walls of the Royal Dock, the new fish dock lock and extensions to the fish dock pontoon, a graving dock and a further fish dock, a connecting cut between the Royal Dock and the Old Dock and finally the West Marsh Dock. In the late stages of the work Charles Hemingway joined his father, James, "In October 1878 I went to join my father on the works at Grimsby. I had a busy time and learned a lot of valuable information that I found most useful in later life. The ground at Grimsby was very bad to work. It was 80 feet down before we got a solid foundation, alluvial deposits all the way. We excavated trenches 40 feet deep and then drove piles over the bottom, 40 feet long. On this we placed capsills of whole timber and six inch planking on top of that. On this the dock wall is built. So soft was the muck that the bottom used to squeeze up with the outside pressure and the men had to stand on planks to clear away the muck as it rose whilst the capsills and planking were put on the pile heads. I have never seen anything so bad since. My father knew how to handle the job and had a splendid staff of experienced men, timbermen, pile-drivers, navvies and masons, led by Israel Collins ('Whistler Dick' the men called him), who was one of the finest gangers I ever came across".

The construction of the Royal Dock c1850. *From a painting at the Institution of Civil Engineers.*

Grimsby Town station in 1855 with J. Read, Postmaster; E. H. Clarke, Locomotive Department and Mr Robinson, Stationmaster on platform 1.

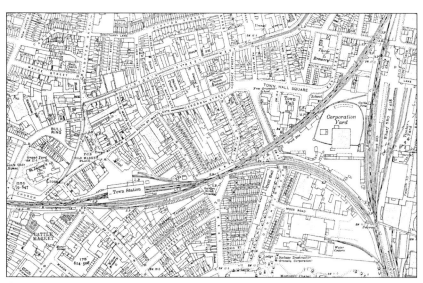

As this map shows, Grimsby Town station was quite severely restricted by busy level crossings at both ends. The East Lincolnshire line runs off at the bottom right, the line to the docks and Cleethorpes runs in the opposite direction.

8

GRIMSBY TOWN STATION

Initially Grimsby Town station was made up of substantial, practical rather than overtly ornate, buildings. lt was served by two platforms with a bay at the eastern end of platform 1, which served the Louth motor trains and was later used for parcels traffic. The station had an overall roof with three tracks laid through, the centre line being used for carriage storage. By the turn of the century a third platform had been added, creating, with platform 2, an island platform. Avoiding lines used by goods and excursion traffic were laid around the outside of platform 3. It became practice in GCR days for GCR trains to Cleethorpes to use platform 1 and up trains to use platform 3, and occasionally platform 2. Trains for the GNR used platform 2 for both up and down trains.

The station lay between two level crossings - Garden Street to the east and Wellowgate to the west, which effectively restricted the station to an overall length of 288 yards. The result was that several trains a day, notably the Cleethorpes-Kings Cross service, would block one of the crossings while standing in the station.

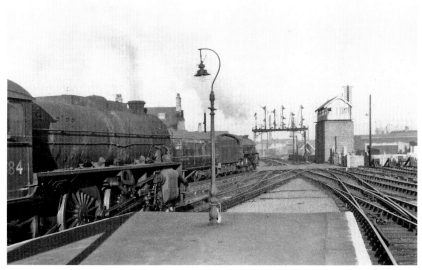

A class B1 4-6-0 leaves Grimsby Town station with a train for Cleethorpes while another member of the class wait to depart platform 2 with a London bound train, on Wednesday 30th September, 1959. Note Garden Street signal box and the impressive gantry of signals. *A. C. Ingram*

Coming off the Louth to Grimsby line, the train takes the left curve to enter Grimsby Town station. GNR Goods Yard is to the right of Goods Junction Signal Box.

Grimsby Town station seen from Garden Street signal box on 13th October, 1956. The 12.15 pm passenger train to Kings Cross stands in platform 2. A K3 2-6-0 runs round the back of platform 3 on its way to or from the docks. The carriage siding is seen in front of the Yarborough Hotel with St James church beyond.

ENGINE SHED AND PILOTS

To service railway activity in the area an engine shed was opened on the east side of the main line, south of Grimsby Docks station. It was a substantial six-road building with a coaling stage and a 45ft 10in turntable. The shed's responsibility, particularly for main line work, diminished when a new shed was opened at Immingham in 1912. Nevertheless as an important sub-shed, it kept its shunting engines, which at one time were responsible for eighteen pilot turns. The shed was half demolished leaving three roads in the open. By the 1950s the rest of the roof had gone, together with the coal stage, leaving the west wall with the offices along it. In mid-1955 the usual compliment at the shed was three class J63s and fourteen class J94s.

When diesel shunters first appeared at Immingham, in 1954/5, they were virtually kept at the parent shed, but before long it was usual to find four outstationed at Grimsby. As diesel power increased at the expense of steam power Grimsby shed closed circa 1957. It remained in use as a stabling point and, during 1959, there were six diesels stabled there. In 1960 it was reported that the shed had been abandoned, however the office remained as a signing-on point until 1986.

Former Immingham engineman Tony Jones provided details of the Grimsby Area pilot duties during the late 1950s early 1960s:

No 1: 24 hour duty, working East Marsh Sidings.

No 2: 4.00 pm to 11.55pm Monday-Saturday, worked Pasture Street GNR goods yard, East Marsh Sidings and Holles Street Coal Sidings. Trips as required.

No 3: Same as No 1.

No 4: 4.00am to midnight. Worked Pasture Street GNR goods yard and at Holles Street and also served T. G. Tickler's jam factory.

No 5: 24 hour duty. Worked the east side of the Royal Dock dealing with general cargo, including butter boats from the Continent.

No 6: A 24 hour duty. Worked the west side of the Royal Dock, shunting empties off the coal hoist and servicing the quayside and Doig's shipyard.

Nos 7 and 8: Both 24 hour duties. The signing-on point was Tank House, Adam Smith Street; duties were at Great Coates No 2 Yard and also shunting the timber yards and Dixon's Paper Mill.

No 9: 24 hour duty; Worked Brickpit Sidings loading up the coal hoists, servicing Titan's Fish Meal and Ciba's factories, at busy times, this pilot was sometimes supported by another one No 9X.

No 10: Fish Dock pilot. Worked north end 6.00am to 10.00pm.

No 11: Fish Dock pilot. 6.00am to 10.00pm. Used for attaching fish vans to the rear of passenger trains at Grimsby Docks station.

No 12: 24 hour duty. Serviced the area around Henderson's Jetty and at night worked the fish empties from New Clee.

No 13: 24 hour duty. Worked New Clee Sidings and shunted the coal hoists which bunkered the trawling fleet (in the days of steam trawlers considerable quantities of bunker coal had been brought in by rail but by the early 1960s diesel powered trawlers had largely taken over, so the quantities of bunker coal were much reduced).

No 14: Did not operate.

No 15. Trip pilot duties, 8.00am to midnight. Worked as required between West Marsh, West Bank, across the Royal Dock swing bridge to East Marsh NS also Pasture Street GNR Goods and New Clee.

No 16: The same trip pilot duties as No 15 but was a 24 hour duty.

No 17: This turn had been discontinued by 1961 but had been the same as No 13.

No 18: 24 hour duty. Worked at West Marsh shunting pulp for Dixons Paper Mill and servicing Laporte's factory.

No 19: 24 hour duty. Grimsby Town Station pilot.

By the winter of 1959 the engines for Nos 2, 4, 6, 10, 11 and 15 duties were usually stabled at the old Grimsby shed.

Grimsby Shed, 17th July, 1938. The left-hand pitched roof removed. The loco is a class J63 0-6-0 T used to shunt the docks. The wagon used to coal the engines stands in the road next to the engine near the telegraph pole.

Class K3 2-6-0 No 61891 with a B16 4-6-0 and a J63 0-6-0T at Grimsby loco 31st March, 1956. *J. Willerton*

Class B1 4-6-0 No 61297 with a Bradford-Cleethorpes excursion train passes through Grimsby Docks station and approaches Cleethorpe Road crossing and Cleethorpe Road Junction signal box. *T. Booth*

Class K3 2-6-0 No 61960 in immaculate condition at Holme Street with the Banbury Fish on 11th May, 1959. *J. Willerton*

GCR class 8 (LNER B5) 4-6-0 No 1068 with a train of fish empties at Rothley in 1922.

FISH TRAINS

An article in the Railway Magazine in 1902 described the Grimsby fish traffic; "About half of the town's 63,000 population is said to be dependent on the fishing industry and the fishing fleet, which numbers between 500 and 600 vessels, gives employment to some 5,000 hands.

The quays all along one side of the two fish docks are covered over the whole of their width and the side next to the water, save for frequent gaps, is boarded-in. A lengthy shed is thus formed, of which the land side is left open; here numerous lengths of rail are laid, which enables fish trains to be drawn alongside, the level of the roadway being sufficiently below that of the fish pontoon as to bring the floors of the vans flush with the flags of the pontoon. On these flags the fish is sold and bought, so that it will be seen that a distance of only a few feet have to be traversed in transferring fish from the trawler to the train.

One by one the trawlers steam slowly up to No 1 Dock, squeeze through the narrow gateway and take their position in the long line of vessels that are moored stem on, to the pontoon quay. The operation of unloading the fish depends on the nature of the cargos. If the vessel has come off a lengthy voyage with salted fish, the latter will be hauled off and wheeled into the market and laid out for inspection. But if the fish is still living and is intended for sale as fresh killed fish it has to be despatched with a mallet before it can be off-loaded. The luckless creatures are hauled up in a long handled net, pitched onto the deck, in a struggling, flapping mass, and are promptly knocked on the head by two or three brawny hands. The fish killed, the catch is transferred to the pontoon and arranged in neat rows, according to size, the finest being placed in the front row.

Soon after the business of unloading is complete the market presents a remarkable sight with its serried rows upon rows of fish. The approach of the auctioneer is announced by the clangorous clamour of a loud bell, vehemently rung by the gentleman himself, he continues the deafening din until a small knot of buyers gather round him. Then his oration begins. The fish are sold by numbers, the finest specimens by fives or tens. With a clap of the hands the fish is sold and the group moves on and the procedure repeated. The ceaseless patter of the auctioneer and the mysterious manner in which the bids are made - for not one of the buyers appears to utter a word, or even wink an eye - make the scene most entertaining to watch. Meanwhile the successful buyer, after appending his initials to the auctioneer's book, tears in two a narrow strip of paper bearing his firms name and places the halves upon the two endmost fish of the row just purchased. Whilst the buying has been going on a number of porters with large tubs on trollies, have been busy collecting fish purchased by their own firm.

Next comes the cleaning and packing and loading onto the trains. A few trains wait a short distance from the fish docks necessitating the consignments of fish to be taken to them by light carts. But the great majority of fish trains are shunted alongside the pontoon with the result that packing is rapidly accomplished. The rolling stock is of two kinds: salt fish and the kinds that can be packed in boxes, barrels or crates, is carried in latticed vans, similar to those used for meat, milk or fruit traffic; while fresh killed fish are conveyed in special fish trucks. These contain three deep compartments, or tanks, in which the fish are loaded packed between plentiful layers of ice. As soon as they are loaded up the fish trains proceed through the docks to Grimsby Docks station and thence out onto the main lines.

The traffic in fish increases year by year and the development of Grimsby can scarcely be better illustrated than by a comparison of the figures of 1854, at the opening of the area's prosperity, and for 1900. The first mentioned year saw 453 tons fish sent away; in 1900 the total reached 133,791 tons".

GCR Chief Mechanical Engineer, John Robinson, designed a 4-6-0 mixed-traffic engine, class B5, which became known as "fish engines" as they were used extensively on fast fish trains from Grimsby. They first appeared in 1902, but eight years later ten more were built with smaller wheels to improve their performance on gradients. Like other locomotives used on fish traffic they were shedded at Immingham. The London fish trains running via Boston and Peterborough were largely dealt with by Nigel Gresley's class K3 2-6-0 moguls, eventually replaced by British Railways (BR) Standard class 9F 2-10-0s and, briefly, by Britannia Pacifics.

Three light engines pass through Grimsby Docks station on their way to pick-up fish trains from the Fish Docks on 16th April, 1964. Class B1 4-6-0 No 61023 "Hirola" is coupled to Class 9F 2-10-0 Nos 92038 and 92184. *R. Hockney*

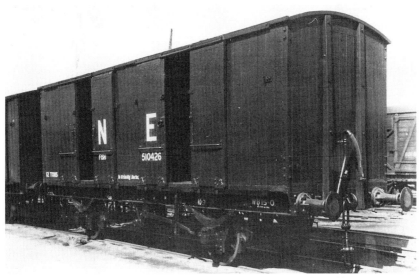

These vans started life as 15 ton vacuum fitted covered vans, down-rated to 12 tons capacity and transferred for use as fish vans in 1923. Most were on a steel underframe but a few were wooden. Some were provided with steam heating for use on passenger trains.

Class B1 4-6-0 No 61190 reverses through Grimsby Docks station on its way to the Fish Docks to pick up its train on 17th August, 1955. The engine was built by North British in April 1947 and withdrawn in June 1965. *D. Coakham*

A smart looking Immingham-based class 9F 2-10-0 No 92194 at Holme Street crossing with a Kings Cross Fish on 8th July, 1959. *J. Willerton*

The Emigrants Home on Grimsby Docks showing posters of Trans-Atlantic shipping companies. People escaping from persecution in Europe would arrive in Grimsby from where they would be taken by rail to Liverpool and onwards to the United States of America.

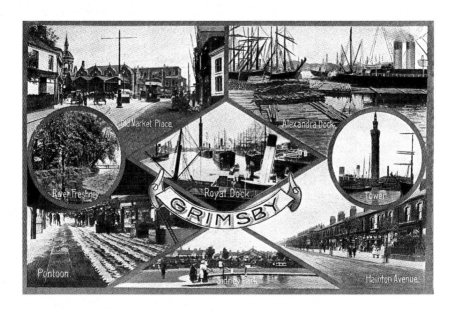

Class B1 4-6-0 No 61264 on the Railway Touring Company "Lincolnshire Poacher" Kings Cross to Cleethorpes and New Holland passing slowly through Grimsby Town on 1st April, 2006. *D. Enefer*

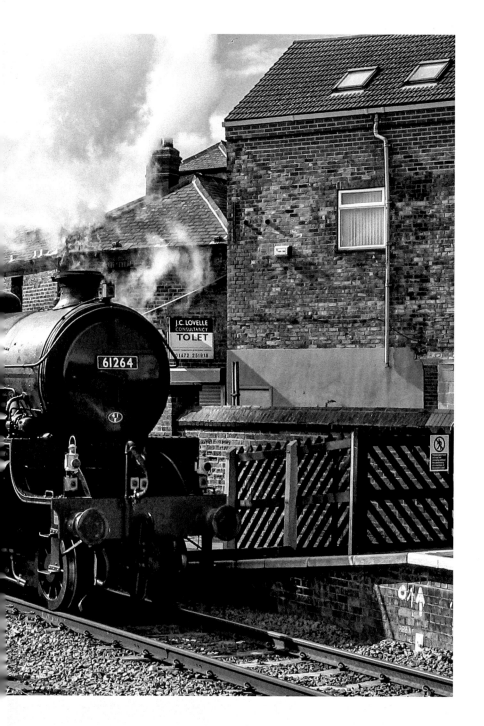

Class K3 2-6-0 No 61829 stands at platform 2 at Town station with a train for Doncaster on 1st July, 1961. The two cooling towers beyond the signal post have long since disappeared. *H. Ballantyne*

Immingham based class 9F 2-10-0 No 92035 reverses through Grimsby Docks station on its way to pick-up a fish train in the 1960s.

Class V2 2-6-2 No 4774 on the 11.55 am Kings Cross-Grimsby fish empties near Potters Bar on 27th July, 1946.

Immingham based class 9F 2-10-0 No 92193 takes the spur to the East Lincolnshire line at Holme Street, with a Saturday London bound fish train in April 1961.

Fish being loaded at the Fish Docks by Scots fisher lasses.

WOMEN WORKERS

As men joined the forces during both World Wars, the recruitment and training of staff became more difficult. In normal times a new employee had ample opportunities to become acquainted with his job, usually spending a period of time in the lower grades working alongside an experienced hand. But under war conditions it became apparent that not enough men would be available from the starting grades to fill the vacancies for the higher ones. The only substantial labour force available was the country's women. Their recruitment helped to relieve a very difficult situation. They were employed in nearly 250 different railway grades, including such diverse jobs as concrete workers, sailmakers assistant architects, fitters, electricians, boiler cleaners, painters, stablewomen and blacksmiths. They were trained as ticket collectors, porters, van drivers, as well as the more demanding jobs of signalmen and guards.

Wartime female staff engaged in weighing and moving boxes of fish on the Fish Docks during World War 1. *Grimsby Library*

Women porters and clerical staff at **Grimsby Docks** station during **World War 1** dealing with boxes from **Francis Nicholas of Birmingham.** *Grimsby Library*

Women porters deal with two milk churns at **Grimsby Docks** station during **World War 1**, a soldier has his head out of the carriage window and the guard has the rear lamp for the train. *Grimsby Library*

GCR STEAMERS

In 1864 the MS&LR took over a fleet of ships that had been sailing between Grimsby and Hamburg and was granted leave to operate them, not only to Belgian, Dutch, North German and Scandinavian ports but as far afield as Krondstadt and St Petersburg. By the end of the century a fleet of sixteen GCR steamers were sailing between Grimsby and all the principal ports of the Baltic and the North Sea. Boat trains from Liverpool connected with these sailings, dealing with emigrants, fleeing persecution in Europe, on their way to America.

Two 18 knot turbine steamers, "Marylebone" and "Immingham" were launched in 1907, they reduced sailing times by a third, but were not a commercial success, and so, in 1911 they were re-equipped with slower engines, single instead of triple propellers, one funnel instead of two and a speed of 13 knots.

The last vessels built for the GCR were "Dewsbury", "Accrington", "Bury" and "Stockport", constructed by Earles of Hull in 1910/11. During World War 1 the ports of Grimsby and Immingham were taken over by the Royal Navy. The GCR fleet of steamers was called up for maritime duty, except the "Bury", "City of Leeds" and "City of Bradford" which were, unfortunately, in German waters when war was declared and were seized before they could escape. They were returned in 1918.

During the period of the war the two port's capacities were stretched supplying coal for bunkering Royal Navy ships. Often as many as nine coal trains a day made their way to the area from the South Wales coalfields.

In 1935 the, by then LNER, steamers at Grimsby and Hull were put in joint management with those of the LMS at Goole, under the banner of Associated Humber Lines. Grimsby lost the Rotterdam passenger service but the Hamburg sailings continued, a weekly cruise leaving Grimsby at 7.00 pm on Saturdays. As war was declared in 1939 the "Bury" arrived in Grimsby from Hamburg, the route was never reopened.

GCR steamer "Immingham" built in 1905. In 1911 the GCR decided she was overpowered and had the turbines replaced by 3-cylinder triple expansion machinery actuating a single screw and replaced the two funnels with one. This reduced the speed from 18 to 13 knots an hour.

The Dining Room on the GCR steamship "City of Leeds".

GCR steamer "Bury" in dry dock in Grimsby. This single-screw steamship was one of four built in 1910/11 by Earles Shipbuilding & Engineering Company of Hull and cost £41,800. She was 265ft long and 36ft wide and driven by triple expansion engines.

A painting of the GCR steamship "Notts" by Alfred Jansen who was commissioned by the GCR to make paintings of the whole fleet of steamers.

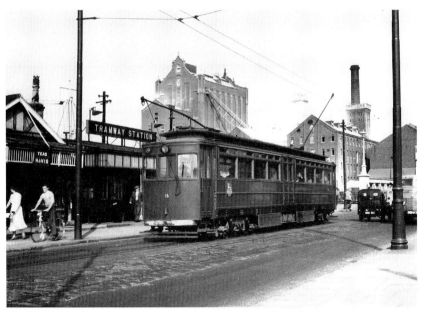

Ex-GCR car No 16 at the Corporation Bridge terminus of the Grimsby-Immingham Electric Railway in August 1955.

The interior of ex-GCR car No 15 on the Electric Railway. *R. R. Clark*

'THE CLICKETY'

The GCR continued to invest heavily in the Grimsby area, buying land at Immingham. A new dock was sanctioned and the Humber Commercial Railway & Dock Act was dated 22nd July, 1904. The area of the new dock estate covered over 1,000 acres and was capable of dealing with the largest ships at any state of the tide. The new dock was opened by King George V, on 22nd July 1912, although ships had been using the port for the previous two years.

Until the end of 1909 the Grimsby District Light Railway (GDLR) was used by contractors to bring in their workers, but the need arose for public transport to and from Immingham. The GCR decided to run a passenger service on the GDLR, using a steam railcar. Two small wooden terminal platforms were built, one called "Grimsby (Pyewipe Road)" and the other "Immingham Halt". The line opened to passengers on 3rd January, 1910, four services each way were provided. In addition the contractor's and workmen's trains continued to run.

The most used and best loved of the local passenger services was the Grimsby & Immingham Electric Railway (G&IER) known, affectionately as "The Clickety". It was constructed as an efficient means of transporting the many dock workers living in Grimsby and working in Immingham. The GCR built the electric tramway which ran from Eastern Jetty to Immingham Town, after reversal the line ran parallel to the GDLR for four miles before crossing Cleveland Bridge to cross the Alexandra Dock branch, and continue the final mile along Gilbey Road and Corporation Road to a terminus at Corporation Bridge.

Tramway services between Grimsby and Immingham Town commenced on 15th May, 1912, replacing the GCR steam railcar service on the GDLR. The extension to Immingham Dock followed on 17th November, 1913. A frequent service operated 24 hours a day using 64 seat single-deck cars. They moved along the country section at around 25 mph, stopping occasionally at one of four request stops. During shift changes at Immingham the trams would work in convoys of six. In 1948 three trams were purchased from Newcastle, and, in 1951, eighteen from Gateshead.

Despite the popularity of the tramway it was closed by the connivance of British Railways and Grimsby Corporation. The street section was blamed for traffic congestion and the line was cut back to Cleveland Bridge on Sunday 1st July, 1956, followed by complete closure on 31st July, 1961, forcing workers to use Corporation buses on a journey that took twice as long as the trams.

The repair car DE 320224, ex Gateshead No 17, with the tower wagon trailer on the Grimsby-Immingham Electric Railway on 16th August 1955.

DOCKS MOTIVE POWER

The MS&LR bought six Manning Wardle 0-6-0 saddle tanks from Logan & Hemingway, which they had used during the construction of the Alexandra Dock. They were used to shunt the docks. The company also bought five 0-4-0 STs from Manning Wardle, two of which survived long enough to become LNER class Y2. A class of engine which was associated with Grimsby Docks for 50 years was the J63 0-6-0 T, seven of which were built between 1906 and 1914. The class J50 0-6-0 T was also a regular shunting engine, and, by 1935, fifteen were allocated to Immingham and its Grimsby sub-shed. They were replaced by class J94 0-6-0 STs after World War 2, when the LNER allocated twenty five of the class to Immingham, they in their turn were superceded by diesel shunters, the first batch of which appeared in 1954.

Class J61 0-6-0 ST No 5278 circa 1924. Built by Hudswell Clarke and delivered new to the contractors building the Barton & Immingham Light Railway in 1909. It was purchased by the GCR in 1911 and worked on the Fish Docks until 1931. *K. Nunn*

Class J50/3 0-6-0 T No 8976 running south on dock lines on 10th May, 1946. *H. C. Casserley*

Class J94 0-6-0 ST No 8069 running to or from the Fish Docks on 17th April, 1947 with the station water tank to the left and Garden Street signal box to the right. *H. C. Casserley*

BRITISH TRANSPORT POLICE

One part of railway history that has been sadly neglected, but was an integral part of Grimsby Docks, is the British Transport Police. Railway police have always existed - originally formed to keep order among the navvies, and, in the early days they were used as signalmen. The British Transport Police was formed on the nationalisation of the railways in 1948. Locally there were police posts at Grimsby and Immingham Docks. The Grimsby Superintendent covered an area from Grimsby to Sheffield in the west, and to Peterborough in the south. The Transport Police included dog and specialist sections, dealing with all kinds of crime on railway properties, including trespass, criminal damage, burglary, fraud and road traffic offences. A wooden hut at the rear of the dock offices in Grimsby, doubled as a parade room and social club. The force in Grimsby consisted of about sixty men. British Transport Police still have a presence at Grimsby Town station.

Building the Weelsby Road subway in 1933. The work cost £20,000 and was carried out by Fletcher & Company of Mansfield. Seen here is the 200 ton plate girder bridge in place. The subway was opened by the Mayor of Grimsby driving under it in a double-decker bus in December 1938.

A view from Newmarket Street Bridge on 13th October, 1956 with a class B1 4-6-0 approaching Grimsby Docks station with a Cleethorpes bound train. *R. R. Vincent*

An AEC Park Royal trolley bus in corfe grey and larkspur blue livery crosses Cleethorpe Road level crossing on 19th May, 1957. With traffic to and from the docks and Cleethorpes excursion traffic this was an extremely busy crossing. *J. Coupland*

Two signal boxes no longer with us are seen here on 24th September, 1984. Nearest is Friargate crossing and signal box and, in the distance, Littlefield Lane box and crossing. *A. Vaughan*

Inside Garden Street signal box, the signalman is operating the level crossing gates in March 1990.

Track being taken up in Great Northern Yard on 25th April, 1979. Pasture Street runs across the middle of the photo and the telephone exchange dominates the skyline. *M. Roughley*

An iron ore train bound for Scunthorpe works past platform 3 at Town station in 1966. Most of the buildings beyond the signal post no longer exist. *T. Middleton*

HOLE-IN-THE-WALL

Peter Clark remembered his time train spotting in Grimsby and Cleethorpes, "I began train spotting in 1959, when I joined the school's train spotting club. Schools offered all sorts of afterschool activities run by the staff - stamp collecting, art, metalwork, fishing, football, cricket and so on.

Most days after school myself and a lot of other lads made our way to Wellowgate level-crossing, near Grimsby Town station. Twenty or thirty of us would gather near the signal box, or next to Kennington's off-licence on the other side of the track. We would see a good variety of engines and diesel railcars passing through the station during the evening - passenger trains, goods trains, iron ore traffic to and from Scunthorpe, light-engines, sometimes several coupled together on their way to the docks to pick-up fish trains.

"Mission Central" for our activities was the "Hole-in-the-Wall" cafe in Brighowgate, opposite Wellowgate crossing. Often when it was raining outside we would clear spaces on the steamed-up window to see what was coming through - "only another B1". We would just about fill the cafe, each of us buying a bottle of coke that we would make last for the whole evening. There was a social element in that several girls were attracted to the sessions, I know of at least one marriage that resulted.

Spotters would be at most of the crossings on the approach to Town station, Littlefield Lane, Friargate, Wellowgate and Garden Street. In Cleethorpes a concrete topped sub-station was a prime viewing site but you had to get there early to get a place. Sometimes we used to cycle along the sea wall to Immingham depot and sneak round with our books and cameras.

Most of us belonged a local railway society that arranged bus trips to railway works and loco sheds, these were usually well supported. Regular groups of spotters also went on excursions from Grimsby to Retford, where we would see a large amount of engines during the day, including Nigel Gresley's famous "Streaks".

At Grimsby and Cleethorpes there was always great excitement in the summer months when weekend excursion trains ran to the resort, many of the engines were types we did not normally see.

The sea of white hair at the annual railway film show at the Memorial Hall in Cleethorpes shows that a great many people have retained their interest in railways throughout their lives. I got my apprenticeship at A. Dyas Motors, in Grimsby, with the help of a fellow train spotter, John Witty. This resulted in me running my own business, which enabled me to buy three standard-gauge locomotives, meet the author of this book and become a fireman on the Lincolnshire Wolds Railway".

Class WD 2-8-0 No 90660 at Littlefield Lane, 23rd March, 1963. J. Willerton

Ex-GCR class D11 4-4-0 No 62670 "Marne" leaves Grimsby Town station with a westbound passenger train in the 1950s. Note the train spotters on the footbridge.

Class K1 2-6-0 No 62056 approaching Town station with the daily York to East Marsh freight on 12th February, 1959. *J. Willerton*

Immingham Shed on a Sunday morning in 1963. Class 9F 2-10-0 Nos 92196 and 92144, class B1 4-6-0 Nos 61325, 61252 and an unidentified member of the class, plus three "Austerities" are on shed. *P. Clark*

A work-stained class B1 4-6-0 No 61168 stands at platform 2 at Grimsby Town with a London-bound passenger train in 1960. The white smokebox door straps were a feature of Immingham engines. *R. Conway*

THE PRESENT DAY

The East Lincolnshire line closed on 5th October, 1970, the Grimsby to Louth section remained open as a freight-only branch for a further ten years, finally closing in December 1980.

Grimsby Docks remained in railway ownership until nationalisation, in 1948, when it became part of the British Transport Commission. They came under the jurisdiction of the Docks Board in 1963 and finally Associated British Ports in 1983.

British Railways announced the closure of routes into the docks in 1976, and by 1978 the only access was via the Great Coates branch. A widened Union Dock allowed car-carrying ships into the Alexandra Dock, where a roll-on roll-off facility was provided. From 1975 this trade developed into the largest activity in the Port of Grimsby, rail traffic becoming minimal.

In 1992 the hourly "Transpennine Express" began running between Cleethorpes and Manchester, it was extended to Manchester Airport in 1995. The route serves Grimsby Town, Barnetby, Scunthorpe, Doncaster, Meadowhall, Sheffield, Stockport and Manchester, and was worked by two-car class 158 dmus.

Since 1985 nine trains per day link Cleethorpes with Barton-on-Humber, serving all stations, with a summer-only Sunday service.

Nine trains a day run between Grimsby Town and Lincoln Central, serving Habrough, Barnetby and Market Rasen. The first and the last start from Cleethorpes and all but the last two run through to Newark Northgate, with connections for London.

A Saturdays-only service also operates from Cleethorpes to Sheffield via Brigg and Gainsborough Central.

There is talk about restoring the direct link between Cleethorpes and Kings Cross but, as yet, no outcome.

The 7.55am Marsh Sidings to Louth working, leaving Grimsby Town and crossing Wellowgate level crossing after returning from Louth. The class 31 was in the charge of driver Lilley on 25th April, 1979. *M. Roughley*

Cravens class 105 cars E51284 and 56446 with the 9.25am Doncaster-Cleethorpes train approaches Wellowgate crossing on 12th April, 1983. A very smart looking Wellowgate signal box, with a good display of plants, was closed in September 1993 and was saved by the National Railway Museum. It is a MS&LR type 2 design dating from the 1880s. *P. D. Shannon*